# THIS BOOK BELONGS TO

Love

Love

www.ingramcontent.com/pod-product-compliance
Lightning Source LLC
Chambersburg PA
CBHW081724220526
45468CB00008B/1968
* 9 7 8 1 9 8 4 1 1 8 7 5 2 *